–25–
WOMEN
WHO
DARED *to* GO

by Allison Lassieur

COMPASS POINT BOOKS
a capstone imprint

Compass Point Books are published by Capstone Press
1710 Roe Crest Drive, North Mankato, Minnesota 56003
www.mycapstone.com

Library of Congress Cataloging-in-Publication Data
Library of Congress Cataloging-in-Publication data is available on the Library of Congress website.

ISBN 978-0-7565-5853-6 (hardback)
ISBN 978-0-7565-5870-3 (paperback)
ISBN 978-0-7565-5858-1 (eBook PDF)

Editorial Credits
Anna Butzer, editor; Russell Griesmer, designer; Jennifer Bergstrom, production artist;
Svetlana Zhurkin, media researcher; Laura Manthe, production specialist

Photo Credits
Alamy: Aurora Photos/Katja Heinemann, 31, Science History Images, 49; AP Images: Tabei Kikaku Co. Ltd, 41, The Emporia Gazette/Hal Smith, 33; Bridgeman Images: Photo © Mark Gerson/Private Collection/Jacquetta Hawkes, 1974 (photo), 53, Prismatic Pictures/Private Collection/Noor-un-Nisa Inayat Khan in military uniform, ca. 1943 (b/w photo), 10, Private Collection/Agnes Meyer Driscoll, American cryptanalyst, c. 1914-18 (b/w photo), 7; Getty Images: AFP/John Zich, 56, Archive Photos/Graphic House, 39, Bettmann, 43, 51, 55, Fairfax Media/The Sydney Morning Herald, 5, Fotosearch, cover, Hulton Archive/Keystone, 9, 12, Los Angeles Times/Carlos Chavez, 46, National Geographic/Bates Littlehales, 47, PA Images/Stefan Rousseau, 14; Helen Thayer, 44; Library of Congress, 17, 21, 37; NASA, 26; Newscom: Everett Collection, 11, 24, 25, Fine Art Images/Album, 19, Pictures From History, 29, Zuma Press/Maxppp/Claude Tage, 35, Zuma Press/Minneapolis Star Tribune, 32; Shutterstock: Andrei Nekrassov, 50; U.S. National Archives: Records of the Office of Naval Intelligence, Record Group 38, Monograph Files Relating to the Pacific Ocean Area, NAID 68141661, 23

Design Elements by Shutterstock

TABLE OF CONTENTS

INTRODUCTION

Throughout history, people have traveled the globe seeking adventure and places to explore. During the 20th century, Charles Lindbergh, Edmund Hillary, and Neil Armstrong became household names around the world. Not as famous, but just as fearless, are the female explorers and adventurers. Gertrude Bell, Junko Tabei, Bessie Coleman, and Harriet Boyd Hawes are just a few of the women who climbed, flew, rode, and paved the way right alongside their male counterparts.

From the murky depths of the ocean to the dark void of outer space, women explorers have conquered the world. They dared to dream, to succeed, to go where people had never been before.

I suggest to everyone: Look in the mirror. Ask yourself: Who are you? What are your talents? Use them, and do what you love.
—Sylvia Earle

Sylvia Earle dived 65 feet (20 meters) underwater near Marouba, Australia, to study a Port Jackson shark.

Chapter 1

THE DEATH-DEFIERS: SPIES AND SOLDIERS

These courageous female spies and soldiers dealt in deadly secrets—and so much more! Some organized supplies and ammunition for armies or ran covert communication networks. Others broke enemy codes or went deep undercover. But all of these women knew they could die as a result of what they did.

Agnes Meyer Driscoll
(1889–1971)

Agnes Meyer Driscoll was always interested in science and technology. She graduated from Ohio State University when she was 22, majoring in mathematics, music, physics, and foreign languages. After she graduated, Driscoll became a teacher.

Agnes Meyer Driscoll, 1914

In 1918, a year after the U.S. began fighting in World War I (1914–1918), Driscoll enlisted in the U.S. Navy. The Navy recruited her as chief yeoman, the highest possible rank. She was assigned to the Navy's Code and Signal Section. She was great at breaking codes, but even better at figuring out how code machines worked. She had only been at her job a few days when she began to help develop a code machine for the Navy.

After the war Driscoll stayed on as a code breaker. During the 1920s and 1930s, the U.S. and Japanese militaries regularly stole secrets from each other. Driscoll was able to crack the toughest Japanese Navy codes. By the time World War II (1939–1945) began, Driscoll was known as "Madam X." She was one of the Navy's top cryptanalysts and an expert on Japanese codes. She was so good, she could tell new Japanese codes just by looking at them. Then she proceeded to break them. One of her favorite sayings was, "any man-made code can be broken by a woman." Although few people know her name today, Agnes Meyer Driscoll is one of the greatest U.S. codebreakers in history.

Nancy Wake
(1912–2011)

Nancy Wake, also known as "White Mouse," was the most ferocious spy and resistance fighter of World War II. Wake was born in New Zealand in 1912 and was the youngest of six children. She traveled to France and became a journalist in the 1930s, just as the Nazi party rose to power. She was against what the Nazis stood for—anti-Semitism and racism—and vowed to fight them the first chance she got. In 1940, just six months after she married a wealthy Frenchman, the Nazis invaded France and Wake got her chance.

Wake joined the French Resistance and began fighting the Nazis. She used her free status and connections to get food, supplies, and messages to other resistance groups. Then she began smuggling refugees and escaped Allied prisoners out of the country.

It didn't take long for the Gestapo to hear of the fearless woman in the resistance. They gave her the nickname White Mouse because she managed to escape them every time, once jumping out of a moving train while German bullets whizzed past her head. After this death-defying escape, she fled to England and kept on fighting.

She led her own operation of resistance fighters, which raided a Nazi weapon factory in 1944. She once killed a German sentry with her bare hands to keep him from sounding an alarm. And when the Allies needed a secret force to parachute into France to prepare for D-Day, Wake was part of it.

After the war, Wake received high honors for her wartime bravery, including Great Britain's George Medal, the United States' Medal of Freedom, and France's Legion of Honor.

Nancy Wake, 1951

Noor Inayat Khan, 1943

Noor Inayat Khan
(1914–1944)

Noor Inayat Khan was born in Russia to a father from India and a mother from the United States. The family moved to Paris, France, when Noor was a child. When the Nazis invaded France in 1939, Noor, her sister, and her mother barely escaped to England.

In 1942 Khan was recruited as a secret agent by a British spy operation, the Special Operations Executive (SOE). The next year the SOE sent Khan and a group of spies into German-occupied France. Their job was to work as wireless operators and send secret messages between France and England. Nazis were able to detect the radio signals created, which made this job very dangerous. So dangerous, in fact, that most operatives in France were caught within six weeks.

Working under the code name "Madeleine," Khan and her network of spies sent hundreds of messages before the Gestapo arrested them. Khan managed to escape. Her commanders begged her to leave France but she refused. Instead, Khan single-handedly ran a communication network in Paris for three months.

In 1943 Khan was betrayed by the relative of a fellow spy and was captured by the Gestapo. For 10 months they tortured her for information, but "Madeleine" never broke. The Gestapo realized Khan wouldn't give up Allied information, and she was sentenced to death. The moment before she was executed by the Gestapo, Khan shouted "Liberté!" as a final act of defiance.

After the war, Khan was recognized for her bravery. She was awarded the George Cross from Great Britain and the Croix de Guerre from France.

Josephine Baker
(1906–1975)

Most people knew Josephine Baker as one of the most famous American performers in Europe. But what they didn't know was that this international star had a secret life—as a spy and informant in France during World War II.

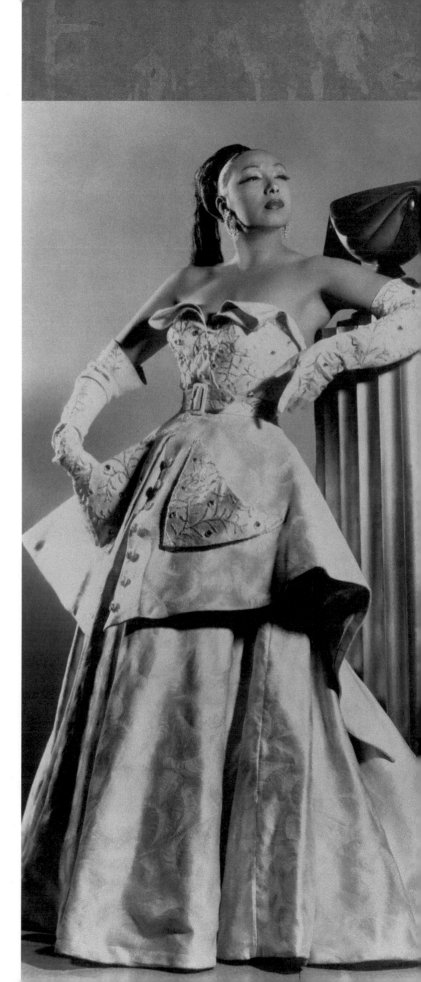

Josephine Baker, 1951

FIGHTING HARDER AFTER THE WAR

Although Baker was an international star, as a black woman she experienced racism and discrimination everywhere she went in the United States. The racism against her was so bad that she renounced her U.S. citizenship in 1937 and became a French citizen. In later years Baker became friends with Martin Luther King Jr. She returned to the U.S. and fought alongside him for civil rights. In 1963 Baker was the only woman to speak alongside King at the March on Washington.

Josephine Baker, 1945

Baker was born into poverty in St. Louis, Missouri. By the time she was 17, she had worked her way onto the Broadway stage as a chorus dancer. In 1925 she traveled to France, wowing audiences with her beauty and charisma. The audiences at her shows were often fully booked, and she soon became one of the highest-paid performers in Europe. For years she enjoyed the life of the rich and famous.

When World War II began in 1939 Baker started working for the Red Cross. One day, a member of the French Resistance approached her with a job offer: to become a spy for France. Baker didn't hesitate. "France made me who I am," she said.

"Parisians gave me their hearts, and I am ready to give them my life."

Her fame became her cover. She mingled with Nazi officers and foreign ambassadors at after-show parties, eavesdropping on their conversations. She smuggled secret messages written in invisible ink on her sheet music. She continued to travel and perform throughout the war. The Nazis never suspected that the beautiful dancer was a dangerous spy.

After the war, the French government awarded Baker the Croix de Guarre and the Medal of Resistance for her courage.

The things we love truly stay with us always, locked in our hearts as long as life remains.
–Josephine Baker

Stella Rimington studying a decoding machine, 2003

Stella Rimington
(1935–)

Stella Rimington was born in England just as World War II was rumbling through Europe. Her father's work in the steel industry took the family to English towns targeted by German bombers. Instead of making her scared, these harrowing experiences gave her a hunger for excitement and adventure.

After college, Rimington and her husband moved to India, where she took a part-time job as a clerk for a local representative of MI5, the British spy organization. Her first assignment was to collect information on MI5 spies to input into the MI5 database. At the time, all MI5 spies were men, but Rimington soon discovered she was just as smart—sometimes smarter—than many of them. When she moved back to London in 1969, she decided it would be a lot more fun to be a spy herself.

MI5 hired Rimington as a junior assistant officer, but she became a spy shortly after. One of Rimington's early missions was to identify and catch Russian spies and keep them from stealing British secrets. Her skills caught the attention of the higher-ups at MI5 and she was promoted to section chief.

Rimington discovered she had a talent for getting people to trust her. "Women make the best spies," she said during an interview, "because they can combine sympathy with a ruthless streak." She worked counterterrorism and counterespionage missions and eventually became the director of those divisions.

In 1992 Rimington became Director-General of MI5, the first woman to run Britain's national intelligence agency. She was also the first MI5 director to be publicly named. Before this, the MI5 director was always kept secret for security reasons. For the first time Rimington's friends and family knew what her secret job really was.

Rimington retired from MI5 in 1996. Today she is one of the directors of the International Spy Museum in Washington, D.C. She's also a successful author, using her own spy experience to write espionage novels.

I have always said and thought that the great strength of an intelligence organisation was their record keeping and their ability to know what they know.

–Stella Rimington

Chapter 2

THE SKY'S THE LIMIT: AVIATORS AND ASTRONAUTS

Almost as soon as the Wright brothers flew the first airplane in 1903, women learned to fly. These fearless female fliers dared to soar into the history books, smashing aviation records for many years.

Harriet Quimby
(1875–1912)

Harriet Quimby soared into the sky only eight years after the Wright brothers flew the first airplane. This was a time when no woman—and very few men—had ever flown a plane.

Harriet Quimby in her aviation suit, 1911

Quimby lived in Arcadia Township, Michigan. In 1903 she moved to New York City and became a star travel writer and photographer for *Leslie's*, a popular magazine. After watching an airplane race, Quimby said, "I believe I can do it myself, and I think I will." Word got out that a woman was going to aviation school. At the time it was thought that flying was too dangerous for women. Quimby proved to have a real talent for flying and for understanding the mechanics of flight. In 1911 she achieved world-class celebrity status when she became the first woman to get a pilot's license.

A few months later, she became the first woman to fly a plane at night. A few weeks after that she flew across the English Channel. She was the first woman to make the trip. Quimby continued writing articles and performing flying exhibitions and her fame grew.

In July 1912 Quimby took a passenger on a 20-minute sunset ride as 5,000 people watched. As they headed back, Quimby's plane suddenly tipped dangerously forward. The horrified spectators watched Quimby and her passenger, William Willard, fall from the plane and plummet to their deaths. Some blamed mechanical error. Others felt that the accident proved women were too weak to fly. But Quimby showed the world that women could fly and could do so with skill and bravery.

> *There is no reason why the aeroplane should not open up a fruitful occupation for women.*
> –Harriet Quimby

Bessie Coleman, 1920

Bessie Coleman
(1892–1926)

Bessie Coleman grew up in a family of 13 children in Atlanta, Texas. She helped her mother pick cotton and wash clothes for money. When Coleman was 23 years old, she attended Langston Industrial College in Oklahoma. She could only afford one semester, so she dropped out and moved to Chicago, Illinois, to live with her brother John. Coleman had big dreams. She loved reading stories of daring pilots who were coming home from World War I. The idea of flying grabbed her imagination. When her brother told her a black woman would never fly, Coleman laughed. "That's it," she said. "You just called it for me." She was going to fly, and no one would stop her.

Coleman applied to flight schools in the United States, but because she was a black woman and schools were segregated, no schools accepted her. She refused to be defeated. Coleman found out that French schools would accept her, so she saved her money and went to France. She was accepted into the most famous flight school in France.

After Coleman graduated in 1921, she returned to the U.S. She hoped to get a job as a pilot, but faced racism and rejection. Not one to back down, she put together her own air show. Dubbed "Queen Bess," she was soon performing for sold-out crowds.

All the money she raised went toward her biggest dream: a flight school for African Americans.

On April 30, 1926, Coleman and her mechanic were in the air, scouting for a good spot for her next air show. The plane suddenly nose-dived and flipped in the air. Coleman was thrown from the plane and killed. Her mechanic also died.

Coleman died but her dream didn't. Four years later, an African American pilot, William J. Powell, opened the Bessie Coleman Aero Club in Los Angeles, California. Every year since 1931, pilots fly over Coleman's grave in Chicago on the anniversary of her death and drop flowers to honor her.

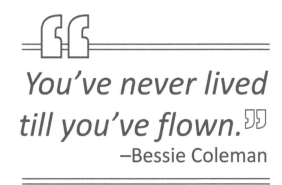

You've never lived till you've flown.
—Bessie Coleman

HAMMOND·Y

DEPARTMENT OF COMMERCE

BUREAU OF AIR COMMERCE

Amelia Earhart in a Department of Commerce airplane in 1936

Amelia Earhart
(1897–disappeared July 2, 1937)

Amelia Earhart saw an airplane for the first time when she was 10 years old, but she wasn't impressed. She thought it "looked like rusty wire and wood."

When she was 23, she took her first airplane ride. "By the time I had got two or three hundred feet off the ground," she remembered, "I knew I had to fly."

Earhart took her first flying lesson on January 3, 1921. Then she started saving money to buy her own airplane. Shortly after, she set her first record, the highest altitude achieved by a woman—14,000 feet (4,267 meters). A few years later, in 1928, Earhart got an invitation that changed her life: to be the first woman to fly across the Atlantic Ocean. Earhart and two male pilots, Lou Gordon and Wilmer Shultz, completed the historic flight in 20 hours 40 minutes.

That flight made Earhart a worldwide celebrity. Next, Earhart broke records as the first woman to fly solo across the Atlantic Ocean. She came home to a parade in New York City in her honor. She became the first person to fly solo over the Pacific Ocean, taking off from Hawaii to the United States' mainland. She was the first woman to fly solo across the United States. She wrote articles, supported women's organizations, lectured about aviation safety, and published books about her experiences.

In 1937 Earhart set out to become the first woman to fly around the world. Earhart and her co-pilot Fred Noonan started their epic world flight on June 1, 1937. On July 2 the Coast Guard lost radio contact with them as they flew over the Pacific Ocean. A massive air and sea search took place, the largest in U.S. history, but they couldn't find Earhart and Noonan. On July 19 they were declared lost at sea.

Over the years thousands of would-be detectives have combed through old records. They hope to find a clue as to what became of the world's most famous female pilot. Did Earhart run out of gas and crash into the ocean? Did she and Noonan survive on an uncharted island until they died of hunger and thirst? Were they captured and executed as spies? For now, Earhart's fate is still a mystery.

In 2017 an Earhart researcher named Les Kinney found an old photo in the U.S. National Archives. It shows a group of people on a dock on a South Pacific island. Kinney believes that two of the people are Earhart and Noonan and that the photo is proof that they survived their crash. Their faces are fuzzy, but many experts agree that the photo is likely to be real. Others argue that there's no way the photo is of Earhart and Noonan. Is it really them? Or is it just a photo of a group of people on a remote island?

DOES THIS PICTURE PROVE EARHART SURVIVED?

Jacqueline Cochran standing next to an F-51 Mustang airplane in 1948

Jacqueline Cochran
(1906–1980)

Jacqueline Cochran grew up poor. As a child she worked in a factory and cooked and cleaned for local families. When she was 10, she got a job at a beauty parlor and quickly learned how the complicated wave machines, a machine that curled hair so the curls lasted for up to six months, worked. By the time she was 22 she had made a name for herself as a talented beautician.

During a visit to Miami in 1932, she met Floyd Odlum, a rich businessman. She told him about her dream to sell cosmetics around the country, and he replied that she "would need wings" to do that. Suddenly Cochran knew that she wanted to fly.

Cochran immediately enrolled in flight school. She soon discovered she had a talent for understanding the mechanics of airplanes. Most flight students earned their license in three months, but Cochran got hers in only three weeks. She practiced endlessly to master difficult flying moves and emergency landings. She entered her first air race in 1934 and lost spectacularly, but she was hooked on speed and never looked back.

Jacqueline Cochran with her speed plane, the Seversky Pursuit, in 1939

When World War II began, Cochran saw an opportunity for women pilots. In 1941 she became the first woman to fly a bomber across the North Atlantic Ocean. In 1943 she helped create the Woman's Air Force Service Pilots (WASP) program. Cochran was the first woman to receive the Distinguished Service Medal for her work during the war.

Cochran continued to break records after the war. In 1950 she was named Aviatrix of the Decade and in 1953 she set world speed records and became the first woman to break the sound barrier. She was the first woman to land a jet on an aircraft carrier and the first woman to break Mach 2, flying twice as fast as the speed of sound. A fearless pilot, she was inducted into the Aviation Hall of Fame and the Society of Experimental Test Pilots in 1971. When she died in 1980, Cochran had broken more speed, distance, and altitude world records than any other pilot in history.

Jacqueline Cochran and 24 other women trained for the space program in the early 1960s. Thirteen women passed the tests, but NASA refused to allow women into the program.

Sally Ride's first mission was on the space shuttle Challenger *in 1983. Here she is sitting in the flight deck mission specialist's seat.*

Sally Ride
(1951–2012)

Study science or play tennis? That was the big decision Sally Ride had to make. She was a student at Stanford University in California, and a nationally ranked player on the tennis team. The great tennis star Billie Jean King urged Ride to give up science and become a professional tennis player, but Ride didn't take that advice. She became America's first female astronaut instead.

Ride was born in California in 1951. At an early age, Ride became interested in math, science, and sports. After deciding not to become a tennis star, Ride focused on school. She earned a master's degree in physics and a PhD in astrophysics. While she was still a student, Ride noticed an ad in the school newspaper from the National Aeronautics and Space Administration (NASA) inviting women to apply for the astronaut program. I can do that, she thought, so she sent in an application. More than 8,000 men and women applied that year. Ride was one of only six women and 29 men who were accepted.

Ride began her spaceflight training in 1978. When she completed her training, Ride was assigned as a mission specialist on a space shuttle flight. On June 18, 1983, Ride became the first U.S. woman in space. Her job during that mission was to catch satellites with the shuttle's robotic arm.

Ride went on a second shuttle mission in 1984. She was scheduled to go into space a third time, but her trip was canceled after the *Challenger* shuttle disaster in 1986.

The disaster didn't slow Ride down. She was asked to be on the investigation team for both the *Challenger* and *Columbia* (2003) disasters. She was the only person to be a member of both groups. She became a physics professor and founded the Sally Ride Science company. Her company's goal was to encourage young people to go into STEM fields. Ride continued to write books and to inspire girls to study science until she died of cancer on July 23, 2012.

When you're getting ready to launch into space, you're sitting on a big explosion waiting to happen.
—Sally Ride

Chapter 3

DOING THE IMPOSSIBLE: ADVENTURERS

These ambitious adventurers refused to let others tell them how women should behave. They faced fear and death as they battled the arctic wilderness, trekked through mysterious deserts, and sailed the endless oceans alone.

Gertrude Bell
(1868–1926)

With her long skirts and large hats, Gertrude Bell didn't look much like a great adventurer, let alone one of the greatest adventurers of the early 20th century. Her curiosity, intelligence, and bravery took her all over the world and made her one of the most famous women of her time.

Bell was born in Washington, England, in 1868. Smart and stubborn, she was the first woman to graduate from Oxford University with a first-class degree in modern history in 1892. Bell taught herself to speak Persian and in 1892 went to Tehran, Iran, to visit her uncle, who was the British ambassador there.

Gertrude Bell visited an archaeological excavation in Babylon in 1909.

Bell was captivated by the Arab world. Over the next 20 years, she traveled throughout the region and around the world twice. She wrote many books about the people and places she saw. Not only that, but Bell became a world-class mountain climber. She once hung from a rope for 53 hours to survive a mountain blizzard! She taught herself archaeology and the Arabic language. In 1918 the Royal Geographical Society of England awarded her its Gold Medal for her extraordinary explorations.

During World War I, Bell became a spy. She worked for a British intelligence group called the Arab Bureau. She teamed up with British adventurer T.E. Lawrence, who became famous as Lawrence of Arabia. They worked closely with local Arab tribes. When the British conquered Baghdad in 1917, Bell was in the middle of the action, working as a translator as both sides built a new, modern Iraqi government.

After her years working to build the Iraqi government, Bell turned her attention to archaeology. She founded the Baghdad Archaeological Museum, now known as the National Museum of Iraq. When she died in 1926, she was buried in Baghdad, the place she loved most.

Barbara Hillary
(1931–)

In 1998 67-year-old Barbara Hillary received some devastating news: she had lung cancer. The surgery to remove the cancer caused her to lose 25 percent of her breathing capacity. Not only did Hillary beat her illness, but she decided to live life hard after that. She learned to ski and dogsled and fell in love with the Arctic. After traveling to Canada to photograph polar bears, Hillary began to wonder if an African American woman had ever been to the North Pole. When she found out the answer was no, she decided she wanted to be the first.

Hillary trained by running on a treadmill and taking cross-country ski lessons for three weeks. Her strength training consisted of boxing lessons and pulling a sled full of logs. And then she was ready. On April 23, 2007, at age 76, Hillary and a guide skied for hours across glittering ice and snow. Finally Hillary's guide stopped and told her she was on the top of the world! "That's when I went crazy," she said. Not only is Hillary the first African American woman to make it to the North Pole, she's also the oldest explorer to do it.

Conquering the North Pole wasn't enough for Hillary. Five years later, in 2011 at age 79, she did the impossible again. She became the first African American woman, and the oldest person, to reach the South Pole. Today she tours the United States, speaking about her extraordinary experiences.

Barbara Hillary, May 5, 2007

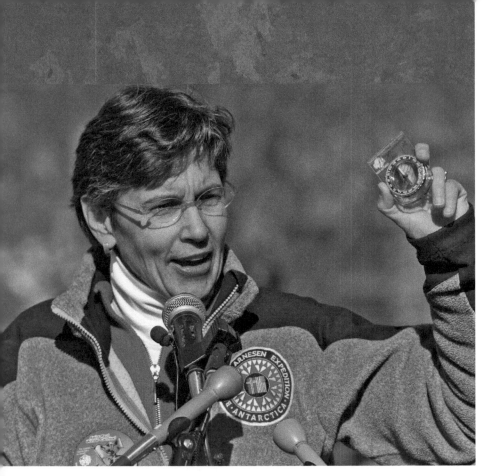

Ann Bancroft held up a compass given to her by a Girl Scout troop in St. Paul, Minnesota, on May 22, 2005.

Ann Bancroft

(1955–)

Exploring the world was always part of Ann Bancroft's life. As a child in Minnesota she loved camping with her family in the wilderness. When she was eight years old she led her own version of wilderness expeditions outside the family home. It was no surprise that she became a world class wilderness explorer. In 1986 Bancroft became the first woman to reach the North Pole as part of the eight-member Steger International Polar Expedition.

The team wanted to get there the old-fashioned way: traveling by dogsled, with no resupply, no replacement equipment, and no extra food. They would take everything they needed—three tons of supplies—on the sleds with them.

Bancroft and the team faced one disaster after another on their 55-day trek to the pole. Some days the temperatures fell below -70° Fahrenheit (-56° Celsius) as they navigated across dangerous, cracked ice. One day, Bancroft fell through thin ice but survived. After getting only a third of the way to the pole, the team discovered to their horror that they'd used up half their supplies. They had to go faster if they were going to reach the pole alive. They decided to lighten their load by leaving behind everything not essential to survival: extra jackets, sleeping bags, even toothbrush handles. Then, only days from the North

Pole, their navigation equipment broke. They were lost in miles of sea ice. Fortunately, they managed to fix the equipment. Bancroft and the team made it to the North Pole on May 1, 1986. This adventure was just the beginning.

In 1993 Bancroft led a woman-only team called the American Women's Expedition. They traveled 660 miles (1,062 kilometers) on skis for 67 days to the South Pole. This gave Bancroft the title of "first woman in the world to make it to both the North and South Poles." In 2001 Bancroft and her partner, Liv Arensen, became the first women to sail and ski across Antarctica, traveling 1,717 miles (2,763 km) in 94 days.

Bancroft hasn't stopped exploring the world. Her new mission is to explore all seven continents within 10 years.

Polly Letofsky
(1962–)

Imagine taking five years to walk somewhere. That's how long it took Letofsky to walk around the world—the

Polly Letofsky nearing the end of her Global Walk for Breast Cancer, near Cottonwood Falls, Kansas, on April 18, 2004

first woman to do it. How far can a person walk in five years? Letofsky traveled 14,124 miles (22,730 km) through 22 countries and four continents.

Letofsky began her epic global walk in 1999, but she'd been dreaming of this adventure since she was a girl growing up in Minneapolis. In 1974, when she was 12 years old, Letofsky saw a photo of David Kunst. He was the first person to walk around the world. The idea of walking around the world grabbed her imagination. I want to see the world like that someday, she thought.

In 1999, at age 37, Letofsky set out to achieve her dream. She began her journey in Colorado and walked to Los Angeles. When she got to the Pacific Ocean, she flew to her next destination. Letofsky walked through New Zealand and Australia, then to Southeast Asia, across India and Turkey, and through Western Europe to Great Britain. The last section of her trip was through the northeastern United States. The whole trip lasted five years.

Averaging 15-20 miles (24-32 km) a day, Letofsky endured extreme temperatures, bloodthirsty bugs, and floods. She lived through a 7.2 magnitude California earthquake, got lost many times, and had days of loneliness, missing her family and friends. But each step took her somewhere exciting and new. Everywhere she traveled, she met people who welcomed her and took her into their homes.

In India, Letofsky discovered that there were very few public toilets, so people would use the side of a road. Once, in Iowa, she was surrounded by a pack of wild dogs. To escape, Letofsky jumped on the hood of a car driving by.

The last part of her journey was her favorite: rediscovering her own country after being away for so long. Today Letofsky travels to speak about her experiences, but she doesn't do long walks around the world anymore. When asked if she had plans for another epic journey, Letofsky said, "No. I'm all done. One lap around the world is enough."

Laura Dekker
(1995–)

Most teenagers have goals such as getting good grades and not embarrassing themselves in public, but Laura Dekker isn't your typical teenager. When Dekker was only 14 years old, she set a goal to sail around the world. Her father, a boat builder, and her mother, a performer, were in the middle of a seven-year sailing trip when Dekker was born in 1995. They settled in Holland, where Dekker built her own boat when she was six. She began racing right away. After a few solo sailing trips around Holland and England, she was ready for a solo sail around the world.

She and her father bought a beat-up, used boat and transformed it into a seaworthy vessel. Dekker named the new boat *Guppy*. Dekker prepared for the trip by taking first-aid classes and practicing sleep deprivation. On August 21, 2010, just a few months before her 15th birthday, Dekker set sail on *Guppy* from the sea of Gibraltar. Her route went across the North Atlantic Ocean, through the Panama Canal to the Pacific Ocean. She then sailed across the Indian Ocean, around the Cape of Good Hope, and through the South Atlantic Ocean to St. Maarten.

At sea, Dekker raced dolphins and watched flying fish jump from the waves. She played her guitar to spectacular ocean sunsets. She battled storms, waves, and, once, a whale that almost overturned *Guppy*. One year and five months later, Dekker completed her world journey, becoming the youngest person to circumnavigate the globe by boat.

Laura Dekker sailing in the Caribbean on January 23, 2012

Dekker wrote a book about her amazing travels, called *One Girl, One Dream*. In it she wrote, "I have consciously faced the fear of the unknown, confronted myself and conquered anxieties and loneliness. I've become stronger mentally and feel on top of the world. I know I will get to South Africa richer for the experience of having crossed 6,000 miles of the Indian Ocean." Today Dekker is still sailing and has started a nonprofit organization with sailing and boat building classes for kids.

Chapter 4

CHARTING THE UNKNOWN: EXPLORERS

It takes curiosity to want to explore the world. But it takes courage to actually do it. These women went where no women—and few men—dared to go. They tested the limits of human endurance, breaking records and making exciting discoveries along the way.

Harriet Chalmers Adams
(1875–1937)

A brilliant and fearless woman, Harriet Chalmers Adams was born with a thirst for adventure. She and her father spent summers trekking into the wilderness on horses and camping up and down the west coast, from the Sierra Nevada mountains in California up to Oregon and down to Mexico.

When Adams was 24 she married Franklin Pierce Adams, a man as hungry for adventure as she was. In 1904 they embarked on a 40,000-mile (64,373-km) adventure to Central and Southern America. For the next three years they went everywhere they could,

Harriet Chalmers Adams, 1908

WOMAN IN A MAN'S WORLD

During Adams' time, men dominated the world of travel and exploration. Male explorers and travelers were part of men-only geographical societies and organizations where they had support and funding for their expeditions. These groups refused to admit women members, so in 1925 Adams helped create the Society of Women Geographers.

"I don't know why a woman cannot go wherever a man goes," she wrote. "If a woman be fond of travel, if she has love of the strange, the mysterious, and the lost, there is nothing that will keep her at home. All that is needed for it as in all things is the driving passion and the love."

traveling by boat, train, and horseback. She took hundreds of photographs and kept detailed journals about everything they saw and experienced.

In 1910 she went to Cuba, Haiti, and Santo Domingo, traveling mostly by horseback. But that wasn't enough. Three years later she set out to conquer the world. Adams visited Asia, India, and several South Pacific islands. When she returned, she wrote about her adventures in *National Geographic*. Between 1907 and 1935, 21 of her articles were published in the magazine.

During World War I Adams was the first woman allowed on the French

When Adams was 11, she caught the eye of a newspaper reporter on the beach in Santa Cruz, California. He wrote, "Yesterday afternoon, Hattie Chalmers of Stockton . . . swam from the wharf to the *Neptune* raft and then to the shore without resting. . . . It was considered a wonderful performance."

warfront. While she was there she took photos of the horror and destruction. Adams was the only woman allowed to take photographs.

Adams was intelligent, witty, and had a gift for storytelling. This led her to spend the rest of her life speaking to enthusiastic audiences about her experiences. Her real-life stories of adventure, danger, and excitement filled sold-out lecture halls throughout the United States. When she died in 1937, she was considered one of the most famous geographers and explorers of her time.

> ❝ I've never ...
> faced a difficulty
> which a woman,
> as well as a
> man, could not
> surmount. ❞
> —Harriet Chalmers Adams

Freya Stark at her home in Italy in 1950. She is holding a dagger she acquired on her travels in the Middle East.

Freya Stark
(1893–1993)

Freya Stark's adventures in the Middle East captivated the world in the early 20th century. She had her first adventure at the age of three years old. She decided to run away from home, and told the mail carrier who found her that she was going to be a cabin boy. He wisely took her home.

Stark and her family moved often before finally settling in Italy when she was 13 years old. When World War I broke out in 1914, Stark was a university student. She quit school to become a nurse on the Italian battlefront. She had a talent for languages and after the war she spent all her money to learn Arabic and Persian. Her dream was to travel through the Middle East, and in 1927 she set out on this ambitious journey. For the next 12 years she wandered. In each country she visited—Syria, Persia, Palestine, Greece, Iraq—she learned the language and local dialects. She began writing accounts of her experiences. Stark had one thing few other adventurers did: a gift for writing about the people and places she saw.

Stark's beautiful descriptions of her experiences filled more than 24 best-selling travel books. Her books made her one of the most famous travelers of the time. What she loved most, though, was the thrill of travel itself. She wrote, "To awaken quite alone in a strange town is one of the pleasantest sensations in the world. You are surrounded by adventure. You have no idea of what is in store for you, but you will, if you are wise and know the art of travel, let yourself go on the stream of the unknown and accept whatever comes in the spirit in which the gods may offer it."

There can be no happiness if the things we believe in are different from the things we do.
—Freya Stark

Junko Tabei
(1939–2016)

Before 1975 only men had ever climbed to the top of Mt. Everest. Junko Tabei changed that, becoming the first woman ever to scale the world's highest mountain.

Tabei was born in Japan at the beginning of World War II. She was thought to be a weak child. When Tabei was 10 years old, a teacher took her on a mountain-climbing trip. Despite her frail health, Tabei knew she had found her true love: mountaineering.

As a teenager and adult, she joined men's climbing clubs and scaled Japan's highest mountains. She started the first Japanese woman's mountaineering club in 1969. The group set a big goal

On May 16, 1975, Junko Tabei became the first woman to stand on the summit of Mt. Everest in Nepal.

for themselves: to climb Mt. Everest, the world's tallest mountain.

Tabei and her fellow club members traveled to Nepal and began their historic Everest climb. One night the team was sleeping in their tents at a base camp when Tabei heard a horrible sound . . . avalanche! Before she could move, a wall of snow hit their camp, sending everyone tumbling down the mountain. Miraculously, everyone survived. Twelve days later, on May 16, 1975, Tabei reached the top of Mt. Everest, the first woman to get there.

Afterward, Tabei wanted an even bigger challenge: to climb the highest peaks on every continent. For the next 12 years Tabei traveled the world and successfully climbed the world's six highest mountains after Everest: Kilimanjaro (Tanzania, Africa, 1980), Aconcagua (Argentina, South America, in 1987), Denali (Alaska, North America, 1988), Elbrus (Russia, 1989), Vinson Massif (Antarctica,1991), and Puncak Jaya

(Indonesia, Asia, 1992). She became the first woman to successfully climb the Seven Summits.

After her extraordinary climbs, she returned to the ground and focused on the environment, writing books and studying pollution on mountains. But she still kept climbing, taking students on a climb of Mt. Fuji every summer since 2012.

Tabei died of stomach cancer in 2016. She kept climbing through her illness, barely slowing down. "I never felt like stopping climbing," she said. "And I never will."

Everest for me, and I believe for the rest of the world, is the physical and symbolic manifestation of overcoming odds to achieve a dream.
—Junko Tabei

Junko Tabei is seen talking to a guide, Sirdar Ang Tsering. Two weeks later they reached the top of Mt. Everest.

Helen Thayer on her solo trek to the magnetic North Pole, 1988

Helen Thayer

(1937–)

What does it take to become one of the most important explorers of the 20th century? Ask Helen Thayer, because that's exactly what she is. New Zealand-born Thayer began to crave adventure as a child. When she was nine years old she climbed her first mountain. Her parents said she could go as long as she packed and carried her own gear on the trip.

By the time she got to the top she knew she wanted to have a life of adventure.

The thirst for global travel hit Thayer in 1986 when she and her husband, Bill, decided to go exploring—all over the world. Together they walked 2,400 miles (3,862 km) through the Sahara Desert, following ancient trade routes. They kayaked through more than 1,200 miles (1,931 km) of the Amazon rain forest. All the time Thayer was thinking about an even bigger adventure: skiing solo to the magnetic North Pole. At age 50, after skiing for 27 days and traveling 364 miles (585 km), Thayer became the first woman to reach the magnetic North Pole alone.

In 1994 Thayer was ready for her next adventure. She wanted to live among the wolves in northern Canada. She studied their behavior and wrote a book about the experience titled *Three Among the Wolves*. In 1995 Thayer walked through Death Valley and the Mojave and Sonoron deserts in Arizona, a 1,500-mile (2,414-km) journey. In 1997 Thayer traveled to Antarctica alone, pulling a 260-pound (118-kilogram) supply sled for more than 450 miles (724 km). In 2002 *National Geographic* named Thayer "One of the Greatest Explorers of the 20th Century."

CHARLIE THE ARCTIC DOG

Helen Thayer knew her trip to the magnetic North Pole would be dangerous. Polar bear attacks were a real threat. So Thayer got Charlie, a gentle, courageous dog, from an Inuit hunter. Charlie stayed by Thayer's side the whole journey. He warned her when polar bears were near and even once saved her life. After their epic trip was over, Thayer brought Charlie to her home in Washington State. He retired in style, joining Thayer on mountain hikes. The loyal, brave dog died in 2007. Thayer plans to write a book about him called *Charlie: A Hero At My Side.*

Thayer is in her eighties, but she has no plans to slow down. "I still have many more hundreds of miles to walk and mountains to climb," she said.

In 1975, after only three years' training, Helen Thayer won the U.S. National Luge Championship.

Sylvia Earle sat by a small submarine used by the National Geographic Society for deep ocean exploration, in 2000.

Sylvia Earle

(1935–)

How cool would it be to be so famous for underwater exploration that people call you "Her Deepness"? That's Sylvia Earle's nickname. She earned it exploring oceans around the globe.

Nature was always Earle's first love, especially growing up on a farm in New Jersey. When she was 12 years old her family moved to an oceanfront house in Florida. The beach was right outside Earle's door. She knew she'd found her true love: ocean exploration. In 1953, while she was a university student, Earle became one of the first scientists to use scuba equipment—only 10 years after it had been invented.

In 1970 Earle and a team of women scientists and engineers lived underwater for two weeks. Their project, Tektite 2, was an experiment in human underwater living. The team lived in a huge underwater structure 50 feet (15 meters) below the surface. Their mission was to study how pollution affected coral reefs and to observe marine life.

Since then, Earle has led dozens of ocean explorations around the world, logging more than 7,000 hours underwater. She's swum

Sylvia Earle (right) showed an engineer algae from a habitat's hemispheric window in Great Lameshur Bay, Virgin Islands, July 7, 1971.

with humpback whales and explored ghostly underwater battleships. Earle even survived being stung by a deadly, poisonous lionfish. In 1979 she broke deep-diving records by walking on the ocean floor, untethered, at 1,250 feet (381 meters). She is one of the world's top experts on ocean oil spills and has led several research expeditions to study their effects on marine ecosystems.

Today Earle is still traveling and diving as the head of Mission Blue, her conservation organization, which is dedicated to preserving and restoring the oceans.

Chapter 5

SEARCHING THE PAST: ARCHAEOLOGISTS AND ANTHROPOLOGISTS

Move over, Indiana Jones! Women archaeologists have made world-class finds, from an ancient city to dinosaur bones. Female anthropologists have made discoveries that changed how we view the past and the world today.

Harriet Boyd Hawes
(1871–1945)

Not many people are lucky enough to discover an ancient city, but Harriet Boyd Hawes was one of them. Born in Boston in 1871, Hawes grew up fascinated by ancient Greece. She got a degree in Classics, specializing in ancient Greek, in 1892. Then, in 1896, Hawes attended the American School of Classical Studies in Athens, Greece, with the goal of working on an archaeological dig.

But she was a woman, and her professors, who were men, refused to let her join an expedition. Hawes wouldn't be

Harriet Boyd Hawes sat next to pieces of broken Minoan bowls, jars, and vases in 1902.

The Ancient Minoan settlement of Gournia is in what is now Crete, Greece.

discouraged. She raised enough money to set off on her own, traveling through Crete looking for a likely site. In the summer of 1901, a man from a small village told her he knew a place where there were many old things. The place turned out to be the ancient Minoan village of Gournia. Hawes became the first American woman to excavate a Minoan site.

For the next three years (1901-1904) Hawes and her 100-person crew returned each summer to dig. They uncovered what turned out to be an intact Minoan town. They found walls, a paved road with a clay gutter, houses, and a palace. The site was littered with thousands of potsherds, vessels, and ancient objects such as bronze tools and spear tips.

Hawes was the first woman archaeologist ever to organize and run a large field crew.

Later, Hawes toured the United States, speaking to crowds about her remarkable finds, and was the first woman ever to speak at the Archaeological Institute of America. In 1908 she published a book on her finds, *Gournia, Vasiliki and Other Prehistoric Sites on the Isthmus of Hierapetra, Crete.* Her work earned her the respect of male archaeologists, and she was considered one of America's top experts in ancient Minoan archaeology.

Hawes died in 1945 and over the years the archaeological community forgot about her. Her work was even credited to her male assistant, Rodney Seager. In recent years, however, Hawes' work at Gournia has been rediscovered and recognized as one of the most significant finds of the 20th century.

Margaret Mead
(1901–1978)

Margaret Mead's studies of Pacific Island cultures turned scientific understanding of human behavior upside down. Mead was the oldest of five

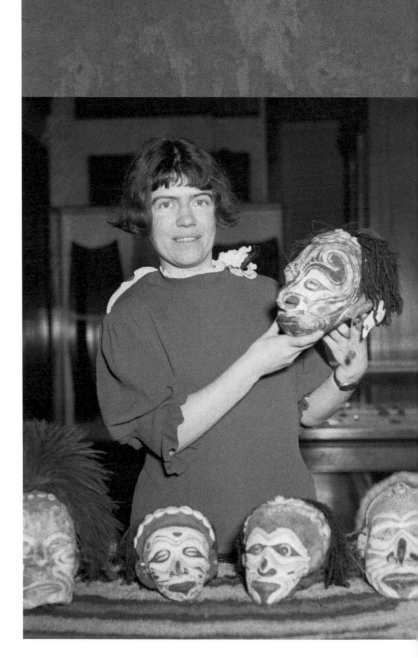

Margaret Mead displaying some of the trophy heads she brought back from a trip to New Guinea

children. Her parents moved the family around a lot, so as a child Mead grew accustomed to moving to new places. Her family also exposed her to different religious faiths, which made Mead tolerant of many different beliefs.

She sailed through college and began studying at Columbia University for her PhD in anthropology, a fairly new subject at the time. Her professor and mentor Franz Boas encouraged Mead's interest in studying world cultures. At the time, there was a strong belief that native cultures were uncivilized. Boaz suggested Mead study the people on the tiny island of Samoa, in the Pacific. It sounded perfect to Mead, and in 1925 she set out alone for Samoa.

Mead's research focused on adolescents. She wanted to know if teenage Samoan girls were any different from teenagers in the Western world. Mead arrived in Samoa and was soon accepted by the people. She ate wild boar because that's what they ate, and lived in a house with no walls. After several years of study, she concluded that the relaxed and healthy Samoan culture encouraged girls' independence. As a result, Samoan teenagers didn't share the stress and uncertainty that teens did in Western cultures. She showed that culture affected human development as much as biology.

Mead published her findings in the book *Coming of Age in Samoa*. Its descriptions of the relaxed attitudes of the Samoan people caused controversy in the U.S., and Mead's work was criticized and dismissed by many scientists. She didn't care. Mead continued her studies of Pacific people until the 1950s. She published many books on their complex cultures.

At her death in 1978, Mead was one of the most famous anthropologists in the world. World leaders mourned her, and President Jimmy Carter said, "Mead brought the humane insights of cultural anthropology to a public of millions."

Jacquetta Hawkes
(1910–1996)

When Jacquetta Hawkes was a girl, one day she found out that her family home in England was built over an ancient Anglo-Saxon cemetery. She begged her parents to let her dig in the yard, but they refused. So she crept out that night, flashlight and shovel in hand, to find buried treasure. She didn't find treasure, but she did find her life's passion: archaeology.

Hawkes grew up fascinated with the ancient world. She was the first woman to study archaeology at Cambridge University. She went on her first archaeological dig when she was still a student. After she graduated, she headed to Palestine. There, she joined an archaeological expedition at a paleolithic cave on Mount Carmel, along the coast. Hawkes and other archaeologists on the dig discovered the skeleton of a woman, one of the oldest human skeletons found outside Africa. This discovery affected Hawkes deeply. She never forgot the feeling of holding that ancient, fragile skull in her hands.

From there Hawkes went on to join digs in Ireland, France, and England, making a name for herself as a well-respected archaeologist. During World War II she put aside archaeology. She worked for the government , founding the United Kingdom National Commission for

Jacquetta Hawkes, 1974

UNESCO (United Nations Educational, Scientific and Cultural Organization).

After the war, Hawkes focused her energies on writing about archaeology and her experiences in the field. To Hawkes, the skeletons she unearthed were almost alive. They spoke to her as the people they once had been. In her book *A Man on Earth*, she vividly describes the moment she found the woman's skeleton in the cave on Mount Carmel. "I was conscious of this vanished woman and myself, as part of an unbroken stream of consciousness . . . this one-time mother of the tribe, who must have lived and died hardly aware of past or future, yet who surely would have known fear, and even sadness, when at last her . . . body weakened and she had to lay it down."

By the time of her death in 1996, she'd turned her love of archeology into books about history, fantasy, and even poetry. Today Hawkes is known for her talent of bringing history to life.

Mary Leakey
(1913–1996)

Mary (Nicol) Leakey was born in England to artistic parents who gave her a love of art and history. When she was a young girl, Leakey saw something that changed her life: prehistoric cave paintings at the Fond de Gaume and La Mouthe caves in France. At that moment she knew archaeology would be her life.

Mary was a talented artist herself. At the age of 17 she joined an archaeological dig as the official illustrator. For two years, her job was to create detailed drawings of the tools and artifacts found on those expeditions. She was so good at drawing that another archaeologist, Louis Leakey, asked her to illustrate a book he was working on. She didn't, but they fell in love, got married, and moved to Africa. Mary and Louis shared an archaeological dream: to find evidence of the world's earliest humans.

Leakey made global headlines in 1948 when she discovered the skull and facial bones of the hominid *Proconsul africanus*. These bones are believed to be more than 20 million years old. In 1959 she found *Zinjanthropus*, a 1.8 million-year-old humanoid skull. This find showed that humans had lived on Earth millions of years earlier than anyone had previously thought.

But it was a find in 1978 that made Leakey one of the most famous archaeologists in the world. The find wasn't a bone or a skull. She

Louis and Mary Leakey digging for the bones and tools of prehistoric humans, 1961

and her team discovered fossilized hominid footprints that were 3.6 million years old—the oldest ever found. They were the first fossils to show real human activity on Earth.

Mary kept digging until she retired in 1984. She died in Kenya in 1996. Her discoveries influenced everything we know about human history.

Sue Hendrickson poses at the unveiling of the Tyrannosaurus rex *skeleton named "Sue" at the Field Museum of Natural History in Chicago, Illinois, May 17, 2000.*

Sue Hendrickson
(1949–)

Sue Hendrickson can hardly remember a time when she wasn't looking for treasure. In 1953 when she was just four years old she found a small brass bottle in a pile of ashes in a wire trash bin. As a teenager she lived on a boat in California and collected tropical fish for sale in Florida. She became an expert diver and began working with teams to explore shipwrecks. During one diving trip, someone showed her an insect perfectly preserved in an amber stone. She read everything she could on amber and fossils. Hendrickson became so good at fossil hunting that she was invited on a whale-fossil expedition in Peru and a dinosaur fossil expedition in the United States.

In 1990 Hendrickson joined an archaeological expedition working in the Black Hills of South Dakota. On August 12 a flat tire on the team's truck changed her life. While the rest of the group went off to fix the tire, Hendrickson decided to explore the area nearby. She looked up and was stunned to see dinosaur bones sticking out of a cliff. The bones turned out to belong to the most complete *Tyrannosaurus rex* skeleton ever found. The team named the skeleton "Sue" in her honor.

The find made Hendrickson and the team famous, but in some not-so-good ways. Questions about who owned Sue the *T. rex* resulted in lawsuits and a lot of negative publicity. But Hendrickson didn't let it slow her down. She returned to hunting shipwrecks and found treasure in a 400-year-old ship off the coast of the Philippines. She also worked on excavations of Napoleon's lost fleet and the royal quarters of Queen Cleopatra.

Sue the *T. rex* was the find of a lifetime, but Hendrickson still travels the world, digging for fossil treasures.

> **Great white sharks, big storms—somehow I think we like to be put in our place by awesome things. Dinosaurs do that.**
> —Sue Hendrickson

Timeline

1868 Gertrude Bell is born

1871 Harriet Boyd Hawes is born

1875 Harriet Quimby is born; Harriet Chalmers Adams is born

1889 Agnes Myer Driscoll is born

1892 Bessie Coleman is born

1893 Freya Stark is born

1897 Amelia Earhart is born

1901 Harriet Boyd Hawes is the first woman to excavate a Minoan site; Margaret Mead is born

1906 Josephine Baker is born

1910 Jacqueline Cochran is born; Jacquetta Hawkes is born

1911 Harriet Quimby becomes first woman to get a pilot's license

1912 Nancy Wake is born; Harriet Quimby dies

1913 Mary Leakey is born

1914 Noor Inayat Khan is born

1914 World War I begins

1918 World War I ends

1920 Amelia Earhart takes her first airplane ride

1922 Amelia Earhart sets woman's altitude record (14,000 feet)

1925 Josephine Baker moves to Europe

1926 Bessie Coleman dies; Gertrude Bell dies

1928 Amelia Earhart is the first woman to fly across the Atlantic

1932 Amelia Earhart is the first woman to fly solo across the Atlantic and solo coast-to-coast

1935 Stella Rimington is born; Sylvia Earle is born; Amelia Earhart is the first woman to fly solo from Hawaii to California

1937 Amelia Earhart begins her attempt to fly around the world; she disappears a month later

1937 Harriet Chalmers Adams dies; Helen Thayer is born

1939 World War II begins; Germany invades France; Junko Tabei is born; Harriet Boyd Hawes dies

1941 U.S. joins World War II; Jacqueline Cochran is the first woman to fly a bomber across the North Atlantic Ocean

1943 Noor Inayat Khan is betrayed and captured by the Nazis; Jacqueline Cochran helps create the Women's Air Force Service Pilots (WASP)

1945 World War II ends

1948 Mary Leakey discovers 1.6 million year old hominid

1949 Sue Hendrickson is born

1950 Jacqueline Cochran is named Avatrix of the Decade

1951 Sally Ride is born

1953 Jacqueline Cochran is the first woman to break the sound barrier

1959 Mary Leakey discovers 1.8 million year old hominid fossils

1963 Josephine Baker is the only woman to speak at the March on Washington

1970 Sylvia Earle lives underwater for two weeks

1971 Agnes Myer Driscoll dies

1975 Junko Tabei is the first woman to climb Mt. Everest

1976 Mary Leakey discovers fossilized hominid footprints

1978 Margaret Mead dies

1980 Jacqueline Cochran dies

1983 Sally Ride is the first American woman in space

1990 Sue Hendrickson discovers the world's most complete *T. rex* skeleton

1992 Stella Rimington becomes the first woman Director General of MI5

1993 Freya Stark dies

1995 Laura Dekker is born

1996 Stella Rimington retires from MI5; Mary Leakey dies; Jacquetta Hawkes dies

1999 Polly Letofsky begins her walk around the world

2007 Barbara Hillary is the oldest person and first black woman to reach the North Pole

2010 Laura Dekker begins her solo sail around the world

2011 Nancy Wake dies; Barbara Hillary is the oldest person and first black woman to reach the South Pole

2016 Junko Tabei dies

Glossary

amber—a yellowish brown substance formed from fossilized tree sap; some insect fossils are preserved in amber

Anglo-Saxon—a member of a group of people with German ancestry who once occupied England

anthropology—science that deals with cultural and social development of humankind

anti-Semitism— discrimination against Jews, because of their cultural background, religion, and race

archaeology—the study of human life from long ago

circumnavigate—to sail or travel completely around the world

counterespionage—detection and elimination of enemy spies

counterterrorism—actions taken against terrorism; terrorism is the use of violence and destructive acts to create fear and to achieve a political or religious goal

cryptanalysis—breaking coded messages without the key

ecosystem—a system of living and nonliving things in an environment

fossil—the remains or traces of plants and animals that are preserved as rock

Gestapo—the secret police of Nazi Germany

hominid—a group consisting of modern and extinct humans and great apes

mach—the speed of an object in relation to the speed of sound

Minoan—ancient civilization on the island of Crete from 3000 to 1100 BC

prehistoric—time period before recorded history

untethered—to release from a tether or rope

Critical Thinking Questions

1. Many of these female explorers and adventurers became known for their exploits during times when women were discouraged from being independent. What kind of negative reactions might they have received? Who might have benefited from their success?
2. Jacqueline Cochran trained for the space program in the 1960s, but she was not chosen because she was a woman. Sally Ride became the first woman in space almost 20 years later. What changed over the course of 20 years to alter the policy allowing women astronauts?
3. The women in this book come from very different places, and lived during different times. Pick a few from different time periods and locations and talk about what traits they have in common with one another and how they might be different.

Further Reading

Fertig, Dennis. *Sylvia Earle: Ocean Explorer. Women in Conservation.* Chicago: Heinemann, 2015.

Issacs, Sally. *Helen Thayer's Arctic Adventure: A Woman and a Dog Walk to the North Pole.* Mankato, MN: Capstone Press, 2017.

Ross, Michael. *A World of Her Own: 24 Amazing Women Explorers and Adventurers.* Women of Action. Chicago: Chicago Review Press, 2014.

Internet Links

Use FactHound to find Internet sites related to this book.

Visit *www.facthound.com*

Just type in 9780756558536 and go.

Source Notes

Page 8, col. 1, line 24: Jeannine Vegh. "Women's Museum of California: The Untold Story of Madam X." Women's Museum of California. August 9, 2017, https://womensmuseum. wordpress.com/2017/08/09/the-untold-story-of-madame-x

Page 9, col. 1, line 5: Paul Vitello. "Nancy Wake, Proud Spy and Nazi Foe, Dies at 98." *The New York Times.* August 13 2011, http://www.nytimes.com/2011/08/14/world/ europe/14wake.html

Page 10, col. 2, line 4: Christopher Woolf. "The Indian Spy Princess Who Died Fighting the Nazis." Pri. February 7, 2017, https://www.pri.org/stories/2017-02-07/indian-spy-princess-who-died-fighting-nazis

Page 13, col. 2, line 1: "Josephine Baker." Biography. 2016, https://www.biography.com/ people/josephine-baker-9195959

Page 15, col. 1, line 19: "Dame Stella Rimington." MI5. https://www.mi5.gov.uk/dame-stella-rimington

Page 18, col. 2, line 6: Peter Tyson. "America's First Lady of the Air." *PBS.* February 22, 2005, http://www.pbs.org/wgbh/nova/space/americas-first-lady-of-the-air.html

Page 20, col. 1, line 7: Thelma Rudd. "Yesterday, Today and Tomorrow." Bessie Coleman. org. http://www.bessiecoleman.org/bio-bessie-coleman.php

Page 21, col. 2, line 2: "Amelia Earhart Biography." Amelia Earhart.com. April 2017, https://www.ameliaearhart.com/biography/

Page 27, col. 1, line 13: Denise Grady. "American Woman Who Shattered Space Ceiling." *The New York Times.* July 23, 2012, http://www.nytimes.com/2012/07/24/science/space/ sally-ride-trailblazing-astronaut-dies-at-61.html

Page 38, col. 2, line 9: Brook Sutton. "Harriet Chalmers Adams: The Original Adventure-lebrity." Adventure-journal.com. January 28, 2016, https://www.adventure-journal. com/2016/01/harriet-chalmers-adams-the-original-adventure-lebrity/

Source Notes

Page 40, col. 2, line 4: Colin Thubron. "Sophisticated Traveler." *The New York Times*. October 10, 1999, https://archive.nytimes.com/www.nytimes.com/books/99/10/10/reviews/991010.10thubrot.html

Page 46, col. 1, line 3: Mary Beth Griggs. "At 81, This Record-Breaking Diver Isn't Done Exploring The Ocean's Depths." Popsci. December 23, 2016, https://www.popsci.com/sylvia-earle-diving-ocean-explorer

Page 50, col. 1, line 4: Brian Fagan. Archaeologists: Explorers of the Human Past. New York: Oxford University Press, 2003, p. 100

All Internet sites were accessed on May 24, 2018.

Select Bibliography

Atwood, Kathryn. *Women Heroes of World War II.* Chicago: Chicago Review Press, 2011.

Elsohn, Michael. *A World of Her Own: 24 Amazing Women Explorers and Adventurers.* Chicago: Chicago Review Press, 2014.

Gibson, Karen Bush. *Women Aviators.* Chicago: Chicago Review Press, 2013.

About the Author

Allison Lassieur has been a freelance writer for more than 20 years, specializing in history, science, the unexplained, and famous people. Her book *The Harlem Renaissance*, was a *Booklist* recommendation in 2014, and her book *Can You Survive the Titanic?* was awarded the 2014 Best E book from Digital Book World. She lives in upstate New York with her husband, daughter, three dogs, and two cats.

Index